IN ISOLATION

Carole J. Gariepy

DRAWINGS BY GARIEPY

outskirts
press

Contents

Dedication

Karen Perkins
for all the grocery shopping and errands
so cheerfully done
" Our Angel"

Ruth and Rick French and family
for delicious Saturday suppers for elderly neighbors

Rev. Stephanie Flynn
for her inspiring messages and outreach
to keep the church family and community connected

Introduction

One cannot plan for the unexpected.
Aaron Klug

This is a book I didn't expect or plan to write, and I was led to it quite coincidentally.

January 1, 2020. I was excited about the looks of the new date. 2020 looked and sounded good ... like 20/20 vision. Gerry finished his chemotherapy and had a good report about the reduction of the tumor and hopefulness about the maintenance therapy offered for lymphoma. I was excited and hopeful about the year ahead.

After Gerry's doctor appointment in mid January and no more appointments for two months, we headed for our son Cort's house in Hawaii. It's located on the Big Island and we made arrangements to spend one week of that time on Molokai, a new experience for us where I planned to begin my next travel book. I did write a chapter on Molokai while we were there, but little did I realize that the experience at the isolated leper colony on that island would soon be followed by our own experience with isolation.

I was so affected emotionally by the stressful life and times those folks faced, and then to come home to the coronavirus, the emotion and stress transferred to us. I knew we had to be very careful. We are both in our 80's; Gerry had a weakened immune system from his chemotherapy; also a heart issue. I always tell new brides that their husband is their first child, and I was feeling more motherly toward him than ever. Mothers will do anything to protect their children.

As the days and weeks went on and we stayed in the house, a place we visited years ago came to mind -- a Japanese Internment Camp. The isolation there was really a terrible one, one that never should have happened and it went on for years. It made me think, "Why should we feel sorry for ourselves? We who are isolating because of this virus are isolating to protect ourselves and others, to stop the spread. The lepers were in isolation to stop the spread. The Japanese-Americans were isolated for no reason, a dreadful mistake.

It happened during World War II. I wondered if any who were isolated in one of those camps were still alive. Could I locate someone? The Internet! I found Paul Chihara, a prominent music professor and composer with a story that should be told.

This book developed on its own accord. For people who like to write, writing seems to be the first thing they turn to when they have feelings to express. It's a release, and it has been my outlet during this period of isolation.

Two people helped bring it to fruition. My good friend Linda Langevin figured out all the technical aspects, and my dear husband Gerry edited every word, added helpful ideas throughout, and designed the cover. He always makes little books for our special needs son Grant, and we've included the one that tells what life was like for him in his group home during the pandemic.

Part I

Japanese Internment in World War II

Injustice anywhere is a threat to justice everywhere.
Martin Luther King

We were horrified when we visited the German concentration camps and saw how they imprisoned, abused, and killed Jews for no reason, other than they were Jews. Those atrocities are well-known today ... and well-known they should be. But, the prejudices and treatment of our fellow Japanese-Americans was cruel, unjust, and not understandable, and this chapter in American history has not been brought to the public eye with the emphasis it ought to have.

We didn't learn about the Japanese Internment Camps until we passed through southern central Idaho on a camping trip about twenty years ago. It's a story I couldn't forget and it's about time I wrote about it. Gerry and I are thankful to Paul Chihara who lived there and has given us an inside view.

Injustice Personified

December 7, 1941, the Japanese bombed Pearl Harbor.
Evening of December 7, 1941, Isao Chihara, Paul's father, was arrested -- with no charges against him.

Four-year-old son Paul remembers the night vividly ...

The evening of the attack on Pearl Harbor, the FBI came to our home in Seattle and arrested our father. There were no charges. They took him away in hand cuffs, and we did not know where, nor for how long. We learned later that he was in a prison-of-war camp in New Mexico. we did not see him until early 1945, when he was released to join the rest of the family in our Minidoka relocation camp -- a changed and brutalized man.

Isao Chihara emigrated from Japan to the United States in 1913. He was only 10 years old. He came here to earn money to send back home to help his family during a period of poverty and instability.

He was the oldest in the family; his name Isao means "brave, accomplished, respected" so he was given the duty to go to the United States and help the family. It must have been a hard decision for his parents to make, and certainly they weren't the only parents making that decision. Many families were in desperate need for financial help. Not only could the families back home benefit but the move gave them hope that better opportunities would lie ahead for their sons in the land that represented opportunity and prosperity.

Isao must have been a competent and courageous young man to take on that responsibility. We can only imagine the thoughts and emotions that must have filled his young mind during the month-long voyage. Not only would he go to a new country and have to find a job, but also he would have to learn a new language.

Paul, like many of us who wished we asked more questions to our parents and grandparents about their history, never learned how his father managed the trip to Seattle alone or how he got his start there. Most likely there was a relative or friend who had previously emigrated to meet him and help him get settled.

Isao settled into Seattle's Japanese-American community district of Chinatown, which today is called "The International Settlement," and soon got a job working as cabin boy for Mr. James Hill in his private car on the Great Northern Railway. Mr. Hill was the founder of that historic rail line which ran from Seattle to St. Paul. Isao did errands for Mr. Hill and was responsible for his personal effects, a very responsible position for a young boy.

Jobs were available for Japanese immigrants, jobs of servitude. Americans did not look upon Asians as equals. They were considered aliens -- people who don't belong. The U.S. Congress passed a law in 1911 that only white people and those of African descent could apply for citizenship, Asian races were considered aliens. In 1913, an alien bill prevented Japanese form owning land. Then in 1924, Congress passed an immigration law that prevented anyone from coming here who was ineligible for citizenship, so that eliminated any more Japanese from entering the U.S. The only exception was for a wife; she was allowed to join her husband.

In 1927, Isao was 24 and ready to settle down and have a wife, but there was a shortage of Japanese girls in

America; young men and boys came here to find work, and they outnumbered the few Japanese daughters by eight to one. So, Isao did what many young Japanese men in America did, he sent his picture to his family to make arrangements for him to have a Picture Bride, an "O-miai" in Japanese.

An Omiai ceremony is a legal way to get married and is still performed in some countries today. Isao's marriage was arranged by his family and their friends, the Fushiki family who had a 17-year-old daughter Nobue. Nobue, like Isao, was the eldest in her family, making her a good choice to be a woman who would be mature and responsible for the venture of starting life as a new bride in a new country.

The wedding ceremony took place in Japan -- it was a marriage of Nobue to Isao's picture. After the ceremony, she sailed to Seattle to join her husband. She certainly had great courage, which is shown at that time and in the years to come.

Nobue got a job as a maid in a nearby hotel. She and Isao worked and saved and planned, and in a few years they were ready to start a jewelry business. They rented a tiny store near the train station to open a business selling pens, watches, along with rings and other jewelry pieces. They worked hard and their little "Mom and Pop" store grew and became well established in their Japanese settlement. Along with the growing business came a growing family -- four children, three boys and one girl. Paul was the youngest.

Isao and Nobue with sons Charles and Theodore,
1934
(Note U.S. sailor suit on Theodore)

Because of Bombing at Pearl Harbor

Isao supplemented the family income by teaching martial arts. He was highly respected in the community, and that esteem along with his skill in martial arts is probably what pointed him out to be a threat to the United States on the day of the devastating Pearl Harbor bombing when he was hauled off to a prisoner of war camp. Decisions and actions were made impetuously.

Were our military and government leaders expecting an internal uprising from the Japanese who lived here, ones who had been here many years and had well-established businesses and a family who spoke and wrote English? Isao had lived in the United States for 35 years, and though his race faced prejudice here, as many immigrant groups did at that time, America was his home and he held onto the principles his adopted country stood for ... that all men are created equal. He was horrified and ashamed of what the Japanese had done in Nanking. Now they had bombed Pearl Harbor and he was put him in prison because of it. He and his fellow Japanese-Americans were hated. He was a man without a country.

What was his wife thinking? We can only imagine the fear and uncertainty and the burden she was feeling. No husband. Four children to care for, Theodore 13, Charles 10, Catholine 7, and Paul 4. Word was circulating that all Japanese would be taken away. Henry McLemore of Hearst Newspapers wrote: *I am for the immediate removal of every Japanese on the West Coast to a point deep in the interior. Herd 'em up, pack 'em off ... Personally I hate the Japanese and that goes for all of them.* Five weeks later those rumors became a reality.

Nobue received a notice with the date and time to be at the bus station, ready for departure with her children.

Internment

She had three weeks to sell their property and get ready to leave, and that allotment of time was actually more than many had; some were only given a few days' notice. Each member of a family was allowed to bring one suitcase.

What to pack? A family accumulates a lot of meaningful mementos through the years and some are cherished ancestral pieces. Nobue had to think about what was essential and she had no idea where they were going or for how long. Warm clothing was at the top of her list, and that was good because they ended up at Minidoka in south central Idaho where winters are very cold and the summers very hot with dust storms, temperatures ranging from -20 to over 100. When she got her packing in order, she went about selling their belongings, a very sad and disappointing process because people knew the plight these folks were facing and would only pay a fraction of what the possessions were worth. She was not able to sell the merchandise in the jewelry store so everything there was just left behind.

Ten camps were hastily being built to house the 120,000 Japanese who would be relocated. The camp Nobue and her family were assigned to wasn't completed yet so the bus took them to temporary quarters in Puyallup where the Washington State Fair has been held every year since 1900. The fair is a gala spring and fall event so the buildings were not being used in January when the Chihara family arrived by curtained bus. (Curtains were drawn, not to prevent passengers from seeing out but so passersby could not see in. Few in the United States were aware of the internment.) Can you imagine what a dismal ride that was -- leaving behind everything you've worked for, not knowing where you were going or for how long, and riding in a congested bus with the curtains drawn? Depressing, scary, and claustrophobic. Paul said he just curled up and slept most of the way, he was spared the stress of the situation. There were some advantages to being a four-year-old.

Each family was given a small area for a temporary shelter in one of the buildings at the fair grounds. Paul's family was assigned to one of the horse stalls. A horse stall ... a small closed-in place that always has an odor! Paul said his mother was stoic. Her strength in facing the unbelievable ordeal she was facing, and would continue to face for four years, was admirable. Living in a horse stable! Japanese people are noted for their cleanliness. Gerry and I can vouch for that from our visit to Japan; never have we seen such an immaculate country. Though Nobue must have been horrified, she didn't complain to her children. Her ability to endure and make the best of a situation, surely had a powerful effect on her children.

> *When something bad happens you have three choices:*
> *You can either let it define you,*
> *Let it destroy you, or*
> *You can let it strengthen you.*
> Dr. Seuss
> (Theodor Seuss Geisel)

They were happy when they received news that the camp was ready for them and prepared for the train trip that would take them there. Minidoka was the name of the camp, and like all of the camps, it was built in a remote location, a place where no one would want to live. Minidoka is a Shoshone Indian word that means "broad expanse," and the place is a broad expansive desert landscape. (When Gerry and I stopped there in the early 2000's, it was a very uninviting place, flat with brush and the deteriorating remains of one camp structure. A neighbor told us he heard that the government was talking about restoring it. The whole shocking story was new to us, and when I think about it now the same depressing emotion arises that I felt then.)

The anticipation they felt about moving to the newly-built camp must have quickly evaporated when they viewed the 946-acre, flat, dreary landscape of sand and sagebrush, the long military-style barracks they would live in, the electrified barbed-wire fencing that surrounded it all, and guard towers at intervals manned with watchful soldiers with machine guns.

The compound was unfinished when they arrived, but eventually, with the help of the prisoners, it was developed into a little village with thirty-six buildings for housing the 10,000 people, about 300 in each building. Paul's family lived in Block 14. Each of the buildings had laundry facilities, bathrooms, and a mess hall, and each family had one 16' by 20' room to set up their home, a single bulb hung from the roof. The village had elementary and high schools, general stores, a beauty shop, two barber shops, a hospital, library, movie theater, recreational field (where they played a lot of baseball), and two fire stations. The camp was managed by the War Relocation Authority (WRA) but the prisoners in the compound not only helped with the construction but maintained it afterward, which was good because they bettered it to meet their own standards of living, including staffing the kitchen with their own people so everyone was able to enjoy their Japanese cuisine. The isolated "village" met the needs of these peaceful prisoners, but it certainly was degrading after they had worked so hard to succeed and were loyal American citizens.

Residents of Block 14

Privacy. There was none. Thin walls separated one room from another, but there were no ceilings so sounds carried throughout the barracks. Fortunately, the Japanese have quiet respectful habits or the noise would have been even worse. (We admired their soft-spoken ways when we visited Japan. No yelling, no using cell phones in a public place, no horn-blowing unless emergency, no loud music blasting from a car or building, even the children were quiet. Such a peaceful country. One time when Gerry and I were in a marketplace, I called to him from maybe 15 feet away to come see some item I liked. Quickly, and very courteously, our guide came over to me and gently reminded me that calling out like that was not proper; I needed to go to Gerry and quietly ask him to come.)

One place a person wants privacy is in the bathroom, but was that possible at camp? Not at all. It was the place where the lack of privacy was most difficult to adjust to. The person who made the design should have been forced to use it. There were no partitions between the seats, just a row of five toilet seats, side by side, backed up to a row of five behind them. Sinks were against the walls facing the toilets, and showers at the end of the room were open also. Another problem was that the bathrooms were quite a walking distance from the rooms, so most families used chamber pots at night.

Once you've lost your privacy,
You realize you've lost an extremely valuable thing.
Billy Graham

Maryknoll missionaries came to Minidoka. What a blessing they were for Paul and his family! Those missionaries were an Order of the Roman Catholic Church that started in 1911 and came to be known as the "Marines of the Catholic Church" because, like the U.S. Marine Corps, they work in rough areas, especially places where there is a question about social justice. Maryknoll nuns and priests saw the injustice that befell the Japanese and moved to the camp to give service and support. Paul said they were the first benevolent Americans he remembers having contact with.

Paul's family were Roman Catholic so having an Order arrive from their church was a welcome happening. The nuns provided what schooling he had which he felt was a good early education, and the clergy gave his mother good support.

First Communion, 1944
Maryknoll nuns and Father Tibesar with children
(Paul is right in the center in front)

Paul enjoyed the communal meals at the mess hall, and Saturday nights were his favorite time of the week because residents entertained each other. Some sang, some danced, some played instruments. Paul had a natural musical talent and performed every week while he was there from age 4 to 7. He sang Japanese songs and the popular American songs of the time, one he remembered that the audience loved was "My Mama Done Tol' Me." I can just picture the little boy putting his heart and soul into that blues piece. The applause and compliments he received gave him the confidence and inspiration he needed to continue with music throughout his life. Little would one have expected that a concentration-camp lifestyle would be where a young boy got the start that would eventually lead him to become a college professor of music and a well-established composer of classical pieces, and music for movies. (I listened to his powerful "A Matter of Honor" performed by the Royal Scottish National Orchestra in Edinburgh in 2019. It is presented with a narrator who incorporates the Internment Camp Story with the stirring music. A very moving composition. I could picture the audience sitting on the edge of their seats as they listened. What an effective way to deliver a tragic story, yet show how people were able to overcome injustice and hold good hope for the future!) Today at 82, he is still composing and teaching college students in music composition for movies.

Yes, for Paul there were some good experiences at camp. He had excellent support for his musical talent. He had a good start in school. He had a firm religious foundation. He had a strong mother who helped the family maintain the pride and honor of who they were. Those are the kind of influences that help a child develop good self esteem ... everyone needs to feel good about oneself. It was a hard start in some ways, yet in other ways it was a start that made him strong ... also feisty, he says.

There was no abuse at camp from the guards, but there was discord among the internees themselves. It was wartime and some of the young men in the camp who were born in America, therefore were American citizens and wanted to prove their loyalty to their country by enlisting in the Army. As the war went on, others were drafted. It's hard to imagine Japanese young men eager to fight and show their patriotism for a country that kept the other members of their families imprisoned. What a blight on

American history that story is! In all, 26,000 Japanese men from the ten camps enrolled in the U.S. Army, approximately 1000 were from Minidoka. Most served in action and some served as interpreters, some as spies.

Division and discord arose in the camp. Some families were supportive of the boys' enlistments and some were opposed. Both ways of thinking is understandable. I wonder how I would have reacted if one of our sons had enlisted during a situation like that. You just don't know until you "walk in the other person's shoes."

The 442nd Regimental Combat Team of 18,000 Japanese soldiers has gone down in military history for its valor; 2/3rds came from Hawaii where only a few Japanese were interned. Almost all were trusted and free. (That's another strange situation. There was a high Japanese population in Hawaii and only 320 were held in detention.) About 6,000 of the 442nd soldiers were from the Pacific Coast Internment Camps, and more came from Minidoka than from the other camps.

They fought battles in Italy, France, and Germany and became the most decorated unit for its size and length of service in U.S. military history. They earned more than 18,000 awards in less than two years -- 9,486 Purple Hearts, 21 Medals of Honor, 4,000 Bronze Stars, and eight Presidential Unit Citations. Their motto was "Go for Broke." They gave their all for the country they loved and wanted it to love them.

It is sobering to recall that though the Japanese relocation program, carried through at such incalculable cost in misery and tragedy, was justified on the ground that the Japanese were potentially disloyal, the record does not disclose a single case of Japanese disloyalty or sabotage during the whole war.

Henry Steele Commager, 1947

The decision for the Internment Camps caused incalculable cost in misery and tragedy, also incalculable financial loss for the Japanese who lost everything. And, the United States too had high costs in building the camps and providing food and services for 110,000 people who would have, and should have, been independent and contributing citizens to the country.

Our leaders must have realized what a terrible mistake they made because they released the prisoners even before the war ended and quickly started dismantling the buildings ... as to erase that act from history.

He who commits injustice is even made more wretched
Than he who suffers it.

Plato

Release

The Japanese had to wait until the war ended to return to their former cities and villages near the coast because it was still considered a war zone. Some families decided not to go back but to make a fresh start in the East. Many went to New York and New Jersey. Paul's family moved to Spokane on the eastern border of Washington and raised chickens and raspberries to sell. Within a year, they moved back to Seattle. They had no home but a wonderful welcome awaited them at the jewelry store.

Your store is waiting for you ... the words of the landlord who rented the store to them. He'd watched over it for four years, and everything was just as they'd left it. Paul remembers the store looking like it was full of ghosts when they walked it; everything was covered with white sheets for dust protection, and then, when they removed the sheets, everything began to sparkle. Everything was "untouched, un-confiscated, un-stolen."

Boarded-up Store

Finding the store saved for them and intact had to be an emotional, unbelievable moment of joy and gratitude. The landlord had no idea how long they would be gone or even if they would return. Paul said. *Our landlord saved our lives and provided for our future. We Chiharas owe our eventual prosperity and happiness to these good and honest people, who were not millionaires or profiteers. They did not take advantage of our hopeless*

25

and unjust sentence, and gave us back our future. They were not Japanese. These righteous people were Jews.

The display cases held pre-war treasures that were difficult to find because manufacturing stopped making many items during the war when industry concentrated on providing things for the war effort. Watch bands, Parker and Schaeffer pens, Bulova and Longine watches, Zenith radios were desirable items they had in stock. Business was off to a good start, and they lived in the small room at the back of the store while getting themselves reestablished.

Paul's family was truly blessed. Most of the Japanese returned to nothing; and, sadly, all of them returned to a world of prejudice and hatred. I asked Paul why such awful treatment happened to them and not to the Germans and Italians who also were our wartime enemies. He said, "It's because of the color of our skin and shape of our eyes." The Japanese looked like the enemy; Germans and Italians blended in. America is supposed to be the great Melting Pot where all colors and nationalities blend together, but I think Jimmy Carter best describes what the melting pot should be:

We become not a melting pot
but a beautiful mosaic,
Different people, different beliefs,
different yearnings, different hopes, different dreams.

When I was a young girl growing up in rural Massachusetts during that period, I remember having similar feelings, not hatred but fear of people who looked different. TV hadn't been invented then so I didn't have that means to view the outside world. Few Asians lived in the East at that time and I never saw even one. Sometimes

I saw a black person when we went to Worcester, and I felt fearful. I wonder if a white person would have instilled fear in someone who lived in a remote African village or in a Japanese town. The different-looking person probably would have been scary for them too. I think of the song that really explains the best way to break down the walls of prejudice -- "Getting to Know You." It was written for the musical *The King and I* in 1951 and tells how a British schoolteacher developed a love for the Asian children she taught. (It's interesting to note that Margaret Landon, the grandmother of Paul's wife Carol, wrote the novel that the musical is based on.) I'll include three of the verses:

Getting to know you
Getting to know all about you
Getting to like you
Getting to hope you like me.

Getting to know you
Getting to feel free and easy
When I am with you
Getting to know what to say.

Haven't you noticed
Suddenly I'm bright and breezy?
Because of all the beautiful and new
Things I'm leaning about you
Day by day.

Paul said he identified with Johnny Cash's song "A Boy Named Sue." Having a girl's name made the boy in the song different; Paul's physical characteristics made him different. The message in the song from the father to son hit home for Paul -- the world is rough, you gotta be tough if you're gonna make it. He thought about the song a lot and it made him look at his situation from a different point of view. It made him strong and able to discard the hurts that came from prejudicial situations.

Paul played "Hot Canary" at age 10

People call a child with Paul's natural talents "a born musician." He said, "Music has always made me happy." His abilities first showed at the camp with his singing performances, and after they returned to Seattle, his father bought him the violin he admired in a pawn shop window. Paul was fortunate to have parents who supported his interests, and when they heard him beginning to play popular songs with no instruction, they realized the purchase was a good investment. At age 8 he began taking violin lessons and at 10 he was able to play the challenging violin piece every violinist aspired to master and every audience loved to hear in the late 1940's and '50's -- "Hot Canary." It was the piece he often played at the USO shows (United Services Organization) to entertain military men who were on leave at one of military stations during the Korean War.

After World War II, Tojo's military dictatorship was ousted in Japan, and America, under the leadership of Gen. McArthur, established a democracy there, a complete turnabout of government. However, back in the United States, the feelings of animosity and prejudice against the Japanese didn't change until the outbreak of the Korean War in 1950.

Korea

We still had military forces in Japan in 1950 and that country became our base of operations for the Korean War. Supplies and soldiers transitioned through there and medical services were given. It was a place for our soldiers to go for rest and relaxation, and also the place for embalming and processing our war dead. Japan was welcoming and helpful in every way. Their faces took on a new look. American men brought home Japanese brides. Paul said, "We went from being the Bad Asians to being the Good Asians." They began to blend into America's Melting Pot. Japanese cuisine became fashionable and people started taking karate lessons.

It's amazing how the news media can affect our thinking. We saw the Japanese with new eyes; we saw them from the inside and they became beautiful. If Franklin

Delano Roosevelt were living today, he certainly would regret his words of 1924:

Anyone who has traveled in the Far East knows that the mingling of Asiatic) blood with European or American blood produces, in nine cases out of ten the most unfortunate results .... Japanese immigrants are not capable of assimilation into the American population.

Paul and his wife Carol

How far we have come! I'm happy to say that my cousin has a Japanese wife who is warmly welcomed and has assimilated comfortably into the family ... also their lovely daughter. Their blood has mingled perfectly. And Paul married a non-Japanese girl of Scandinavian descent ... a fine musician (of course).

Marion Konishi, Valedictorian of her graduating class at the Internment Camp spoke these words: *Sometimes America failed and suffered ... Sometimes she made mistakes, great mistakes ... Can we the graduating class of 1943 from Amache Senior High School believe that America still means freedom, equality, security and Justice? Do I believe this? Do my classmates believe this? Yes with all my heart, because in this faith, in that hope, is my future, and the world's future.*

Ronald Reagan responded to those words in 1988: *... we must recognize that the internment of Japanese-Americans was just that; a mistake. For throughout the war, Japanese-Americans in the tens of thousands remained utterly loyal to the United States. Indeed, scores of Japanese-Americans volunteered for our Armed Forces, many stepping forward in the internment camps themselves.* President Reagan took the first step in recognizing and apologizing for that awful mistake.

In 2001, President Bill Clinton designated the ten Internment Camps to become part of the National Park System, and money was allocated for restoration. 300 acres from the original 946 has been set aside at Minidoka. The former camp automotive shop now houses the Visitor's Center, a guard tower and barbed wire fence has been restored, and a 1.6-mile trail is lined with exhibits and explanations of its operation and camp life. It's called Minidoka National Park Historic Site.

An Honor Roll at the park entrance commemorates the 950 men from Minidoka who served in the military. A smaller plaque commemorates the 73 internees who died in World War II -- *For our tomorrow, they gave their today.*

In 1952, the Senate and House passed the McCarran-Walter Act which granted Japanese immigrants the right to become naturalized United States citizens. Paul and his siblings were born here so they were American citizens and now his parents could be also, a step they took promptly. That act also permitted them to be able to own property. However, Japanese were still not allowed to move here until the ban on Asian immigration was lifted in 1965.

> *In every nation,*
> *there are wounds to heal.*
> *In every heart,*
> *there is the power to do it.*
> Marianne Williamson

It was a long road, a road with many potholes, but they persevered, holding tight to the ideal -- America is the only country in the world that is not built on race; it is a country for all people.

When I think about the pride Isao and Nobue felt about becoming an American citizen, I think of this statement in the Museum of American History:

Being an American -- you can make your own decisions about where you want to live, where you would like to work, who you'd like to marry, etc. It means being brave, being proud of this Country, and being confident that we will succeed. Being an American is an honor not a privilege.

Part II

Molokai
An Island that Wants to Stay Isolated
February 2020

First, I would like to introduce Hawaii. It's kind of confusing because 137 islands in a 1,600-mile-long chain comprise the state of Hawaii, but only one of those islands has the name Hawaii, and the island called Hawaii is the largest of those islands. It's the most eastern one in the chain and our son Cort's house is located there in Naalehu, the most southern town in the United States. (We are so fortunate to have this beautiful destination available for us to visit.)

Most of the islands are very small, only seven are inhabited -- Hawaii, Maui, Lanai, Molokai, Oahu, Kauai, and Niihau. Oahu is the most developed island, Honolulu is there. Molokai, the fifth one in size, held an interest to me since I was in grade school and learned about the leper colony located there. I felt such shock and sadness that the people with that dreaded incurable disease had to go there and stay till they died.

In 1980, almost 40 years after the disease was curable, I learned that the place was designated as a National Historic Park. Immediately I felt a desire to visit. Its story is certainly an important piece of United States history and deserving to be a national park. Finally, this year we made plans to go! Gerry always reads aloud to me and one of the readings was Alan Brennert's excellent book *Molokai,* and after that reading, he was as anxious to go as I was.

Making Arrangements to Visit the Colony

Molokai is 170 miles west of Naalehu and for us to get there we had to fly from Kona located on Hawaii to Honolulu on Oahu and from there to Kaunakakai, the only sizeable community on Molokai, quite a complicated route for such a short distance. But, you don't just book an airline ticket, arrive there and then be able to visit the leper colony. The ticket enables you to visit the island, no problem, but the leper colony is located on a flat 2 1/2-mile-long-by-2-mile-wide peninsula that juts out from Molokai's northern coast, and the peninsula lies at the bottom of a steep 3,300-foot-high cliff, the highest sea cliff in the world. Until recently there was a path with 27 switchbacks that one could descend by hiking or by riding on a mule, but a landslide has washed out the trail so the only access to the peninsula now is by airplane, a short 6-minute flight on a small single-engine prop plane from Kaunakakai. However, you can only be admitted to the colony if you are invited by a resident. (There are still eight lepers living there and they rule the peninsula which is a county and visitors have to follow county laws.) How do you get invited?

Looking down at peninsula and high sea cliffs

Well, getting an invitation is quite a process. (Even when people could hike or ride down on a mule, they couldn't leave the trail without an invitation.) We had to contact John McBride, an Hawaiian man who has a good working relationship with one of the lepers who lives there.

He would be our guide for the day we visited, and it was evident that he had great admiration, empathy, and respect for the privacy of the people there and all they've been through. He applied to the resident for our invitation and also obtained a permit from the Board of Health where they continue to regulate and limit visitors. A couple from Australia was also scheduled with us for the tour.

We have found that some places forever affect how we view life, and this certainly was to be one of them.

Leper Colony at Kalaupapa

Travel isn't always pretty.
It isn't always comfortable.
Sometimes it hurts, it even breaks your heart.
But, that's ok.
The journey changes you; it should change you.
It leaves marks on your memory, on your consciousness,
on your heart ...
Anthony Bourdain

Because Hawaii was so isolated from other places in the mid 1800's, the people there had limited contact to outside diseases and therefore had no immunity to them. So, when workers were brought in from other countries to work on the sugar plantations, their diseases and germs came with them, and unfortunately leprosy was one of them. (The disease is thought to come from China.) By the 1860's about 25% of the Hawaiians had leprosy. It was spreading and people were dying at an alarming rate. In 1865 the king knew something had to be done or their race would be wiped out so he set aside land to confine and isolate patients to stop the spread of the disease. The practically inaccessible peninsula on northern Molokai was determined to be the perfect place, a place called Kalaupapa.

Village with world's highest sea cliffs behind

It was a heart-rendering decision that affected the patients and their families, also the Hawaiians who had lived and farmed on that peninsula for generations and had to move. It forced a change in many lives forever; the ticket to Kalaupapa was one way, a lifetime sentence ... and unbelievably and unforgivably, I think, they were referred to as "inmates." It was a tough law to make but we have to recognize that what alternative did the king have? He protected his people in the only way he saw possible.

We can feel the heartbreak when affected children were torn from their families or when Mom or Dad or grandparents were taken away. We can understand why parents tried to hide a child's illness from the authorities, also why friends and neighbors would report about each other to protect themselves. Fear had to fill everyone. It was a time of fear and heartbreak for the healthy as well as for the many who were dealing with the horrible disfiguring fatal disease.

The disease attacked the nervous system and bodies became numb, loss of vision was an early symptom, sores appeared on the body, their extremities wasted away causing them to lose their fingers; their stubby feet made walking difficult, and most died in 3 to 5 years. It truly was a disease to fear.

The fearful boatmen who transported the lepers to the colony didn't want to dock at the contaminated place so they just dropped the "inmates" off near shore and they had to swim to their new residence and find a shelter among strangers. (Not only were they taken to a prison-like place but they were labeled by a prisoner name.) They were on their own to create makeshift huts or find caves; adult lepers cared for young ones as best they could. Food was brought over regularly and deposited in the same manner, dropped off near shore and delivered by the ocean current . I can't imagine a more depressing and hopeless situation ... having a disease with no cure with no medical staff to ease the discomfort and no comforts or support of family and home. This was the situation for the first seven years at the colony until Father Damien, a young Belgian priest, felt the call to serve there in 1873.

Father Damien was not only a priest, he was a carpenter. He was ambitious and an enthusiastic motivator. He sought out the skills of the patients, and found that there were many accomplished people there. He inspired the patients to apply their skills and talents. Keeping busy is healthy, being sedentary and dwelling on one's problems only makes things worse. He helped patients make the most of what life they had. They built homes, formed a band, put on plays, built a church and cemetery, held funerals for the deceased. He identified with their situation and felt the emotional and physical pain they were dealing with. He was their helper and their friend. Though he wasn't supposed to leave the colony after he arrived, he did leave. He was a priest and a priest represented God ... who can argue with God? He became a voice that arranged for needed supplies to be brought over to improve their lives. A pleasant little community was built. People didn't own the cottages but were assigned ones to live in.

Typical cottage

Painting of Father Damien

Church built by Father Damien and patients

Holes for spitting

The little church really made an impression on us. Why did it have holes in the floor, holes regularly fashioned throughout the sanctuary? The guide explained that when the church was completed, the patients wouldn't enter. It was a puzzle and disappointment for Father Damien until he found out that people with leprosy have to spit a lot. It was ok to spit on the ground when Father Damien had led them in worship outdoors, but they didn't want to spit on the floor in the church. Father solved that problem. He made holes in the floor; people came to church with leaves to spit in and deposited them in the holes. Services were well attended. The spirit at Kalaupapa changed. Lives were short but they were full.

Unfortunately, Father Damien was not careful about his physical contact with the patients, and the disease is communicated through direct contact. When he contracted the disease at age 45, he accepted it with grace saying, "I'm now one of them." He died 4 years later. All of Hawaii grieved his passing. He was one of the 8,000 who died there, He was a man who made a difference and left a positive mark on the world.

Even after he died, his spirit has lived on and continues to inspire people. A new museum will open soon in Honolulu where many visitors to Hawaii will learn this segment of American history and become inspired by both the patients' fortitude and those who served them in Kalaupapa, a place that showed the power of the human spirit to survive despite the most difficult challenges.

Father Damien's burial place is still revered

Life is about making an impact,
Not an income.
Kevin Krus

The Catholic church canonized Father Damien in 2009; he became Saint Damien and a saint indeed he was. He brought hope and a better life to a dying and dead place, hope with the Christian message he delivered, and life with the activities he created.

Sister Marianne came and nursed Father Damien during his end days. She was followed by hundreds of other Sisters through the years who came to serve in the community. None of them contracted leprosy. The Sisters were dedicated to their mission but they used good hygienic procedures. As is often emphasized today, they washed their hands! They used good self care and were confident of their safety knowing that God was watching over them.

Us with Sister Alicia who serves as a nurse in the community

Two nuns are serving the eight remaining residents today, and they said they will remain till the last one dies.

A sulfur treatment for the disease was finally found in 1941. It came during World War II when Hawaii was a hot spot for military activity, so treatment wasn't started until the war ended. In fact, an island located very close to the peninsula was used by our military from 1942 to 1945 to practice aerial bombing and gunnery practice. (There are still unexploded munitions there today needing to be removed.) That military activity had to add to the anxiety of the patients.

Nearby islands used for bombing practice

The drug stopped the progress of the disease and after several months of treatment, it was no longer transmittable. Patients could receive visitors and they were allowed to leave to visit but it wasn't until 1969 that they had the choice of leaving permanently .... or they could choose to stay in the colony. Some left and returned to their families, but many chose to stay. The peninsula on Molokai where they lived had become their home, it was their comfort zone, many still felt rejection by society, and though they were cured of the disease, it had reeked havoc on their bodies and they were not comfortable returning to society. The people who chose to leave were "on parole," another term for a prisoner. They were on parole because their treatment would require continued medical follow-up. It was good to continue medical attention but being "on parole" wasn't an appropriate term any more than "inmate" had been.

Paintings of Father Damien   and Sister Marianne

A tribute needs to be made to some well-known and admired Americans who made well-publicized trips to Kalaupapa to visit and entertain the patients in the 1950's ... the von Trapp family singers, John Wayne, and teenager Shirley Temple. They went there to encourage the residents and to show the world they were ok now ... it was time to welcome them back into society.

No one should be stigmatized by a condition they have and just the name of something can stimulate a stigma response. Today leprosy is called Hansen's Disease after Dr. Gerhard Hansen who discovered the bacteria that caused it in 1873; it was the first step in trying to find a treatment. The name "leprosy," even dating back to Biblical times, carried a stigma. The assigning of a new title is an effort and hope to remove the stigma.

At the end of our full day on Kalaupapa, the guide escorted us to the small plane. No visitor can stay overnight.

Topside

Keep Molokai -- Molokai
Molokai Motto

That title *Topside* refers to the rest of Molokai, the large 35-mile-long-by-10-mile-wide part above the peninsula. 8,000 people live in this quiet mostly unspoiled topside area, 40% of the people there descend from original inhabitants. It is quiet and natural and they want to keep it that way. They don't encourage tourism. There is only one hotel and that hotel doesn't even serve breakfast. They are passing a law to forbid people on the island to rent out rooms to visitors. They say, "Molokai changes visitors but we don't want visitors to affect Molokai." The traffic sign says, "Slow down, you're on Molokai." The menu in the restaurant says, "If you're in a hurry, you're on the wrong island." Their motto was, "Keep Molokai -- Molokai." We were warned ahead of time not to expect many services. It was a true warning, but we loved it. We had the best fish ever, always served with rice and macaroni salad -- a bit high in carbohydrates but tasty. Life seemed to slow down; people were friendly; the surroundings were beautiful.

Reminder on road sign

We arranged for a rental car, which turned out to be a truck, a fairly large pickup truck -- no cars were left so we willingly accepted it with good faith that it would work out ok. I was the one with the driving permit, and though I'd never driven a truck before, I had driven our small camper.

Narrow road with picturesque views

Little did we realize when we headed out with the truck that the road on the eastern end of the island was a two-way road with mostly only a one-lane width, and if you met another vehicle, one vehicle had to back up to one of the spaces that were cut out so cars could pass and some of those passing spaces were rather long distances apart. The road was hilly with a steep cliff on one side and a steep drop-off on the other. No way was it possible for me to back up that truck. Fortunately, there was little traffic and those drivers we did meet were good backer-uppers. I guess my age and ashen face quickly told them they had to perform the task. Even though the drive was harrowing, it was breathtakingly beautiful and the ocean cove at the end, so perfectly tucked at the mouth of a valley with high walls on both sides, was a perfect place to have a picnic and take a walk amongst tropical plants we'd never seen before. I did breathe a big sigh of relief though after safely inching our way back over the same road, the only way back, and we both felt we'd had an amazing and daring adventure.

Aka'ula School
The Hawaiian language that was banned in 1893 is returning. The ban was lifted in 1986 and is now part of the school curriculum in private schools. Hawaii is the only state that is officially bilingual.

The remainder of our week was delightful and relaxing. We toured, visited, and "talked story" everywhere we went. ("Talk story" is the term used on all the Hawaiian islands for visiting with one another ... "Come over and we'll talk story.") Topside Molokai was like a ski slope, very high on the cliff end with lush flora, some found no where else in the world, and downhill to beaches and dryland vegetation on the low end. Wild poultry was everywhere, some not so wild came near the patio of our hotel room and Gerry made the mistake of feeding them, which was fun until very early the next morning when the chickens with their vociferous rooster leader came to visit their generous friend.

From the Peninsula to the Topside, it was an outstanding experience. We talked with a man in Honolulu while we were waiting for our plane to go there. He had been to Molokai and started to talk enthusiastically about his experience there, I said "Wait a minute. I want to write down your words,"

With pleasant nostalgia he said, "You will love the untouched nature. You will see how people lived in the past. The pace is slower, it's so calm and relaxing there . It's a place where life slows down. It's a hard place to leave." If we met someone contemplating a trip there, we could use the same words.

Postscript: Shortly after we returned from Molokai, the coronavirus started its evil march throughout the world. We were about to go from learning about the lepers who were isolated to experiencing isolation ourselves, but hopefully not for a lifetime sentence.

Well, Molokai natives, who don't encourage visits from outsiders anyway, took preventing the virus from coming onto their island into their own hands. When an airplane carrying visitors landed, they met it with guns and ordered them to go back to where they came from! Pilots don't argue with guns. Now that's a Stay-At-Home Order!

Part III

COVID - 19

March 2020

You must never so much as think whether you like it or not,
whether it is bearable or not;
you must never think of anything except the need, and how to meet it.
Clara Barton

The coronavirus, COVID-19 -- two labels for the illness caused by a miniscule virus that viciously infected the world and caused the 2020 pandemic -- the time when we could go nowhere. That certainly wasn't good news for travelers; that wasn't good news for anyone.

Nowhere to Go

But ... nowhere is somewhere. We were in our homes -- that's somewhere. We could go outside and take a walk ... that's somewhere. We could ride in our cars if the outing was essential ... like going to the grocery store or the doctor or a job that was considered essential -- that's somewhere. There is no such place as nowhere.

Only businesses and stores making or selling essential goods stayed open but most of the world closed down. Everyone still had to eat. Restaurants could only do "Take Out" or "Delivery" business. Grocery stores stayed open but had to provide the best safety procedures possible. They limited the number of shoppers in the store and provided anti-bacterial wipes so people could sterilize the handles of the carts. They encouraged keeping a 6-foot distance between each other, and also made 6-foot lines outside the store so shoppers would line up six-feet apart while waiting outside to enter as finished shoppers left. A friend sent the following comment:

> *I never thought the saying "I wouldn't touch him with a ten-foot pole" would become a national policy.*

Lined up to enter store

For added protection, face masks became part of everyone's shopping attire. (Before this outbreak, store workers would have called police to report masked bandits entering the store.)

Shopping didn't hold the same pleasant experience it had previously. There was no time for browsing or greeting the workers filling the shelves, chatting with a friend, or sharing suggestions and ideas with other shoppers. One friend said, "You can see the fear in people's eyes." A heaviness filled the air as the masked shoppers scurried up and down the one-way aisles (made one-way to avoid having to pass an oncoming shopper who may sneeze or cough out some germs). Shopping was no longer a relaxing outing, it was a necessary exercise of getting in and getting out as quickly as possible ... and it was complicated by the frustration of empty shelves and low supplies.

Some paper towels, no toilet paper

No one wanted to shop often and no one wanted to run out of supplies. How long would the pandemic last? No one knew. The shopping answer -- HOARD! Toilet paper was the first product to disappear, followed by all other paper products, anti-bacterial cleaners, soups, frozen foods, rice, pasta. Fresh produce shelves were usually well stocked; you can't hoard those things.

What was the order of business when the shoppers got home? Wash down all the purchases. TV and computer warnings announced regularly how long the virus germs could live on the various types of surfaces -- some said metal held germs for 3 days, others said 9, and they lasted a long time on plastic. There were no clear directions, no clear answers. Anti-bacterialize everything before you put it away! One friend told me, "Pretend all your supplies are covered with glitter and remove it." There were warnings about germs lasting on clothing -- so strip and put shopping clothes in the washer. Most importantly through it all -- wash your hands, keep them clean at all times, don't touch your face! Was shopping fun? No. Was it a fearsome experience? Yes. And also tiresome. Anxiety makes a person tired. There was no preparation or expectation for the sudden change. It was a cultural shock. The world was very suddenly turned upside down.

A friend sent me the following story:

> *Corona virus has turned us all into dogs.*
> *We roam the house looking for food,*
> *We're told "no" if we get too close to people,*
> *And we get really excited about car rides and walks.*

Just going somewhere in the car became a big deal, and it was an ideal time for going somewhere -- there was no traffic, also gas prices were lower. The little somewheres we did drive to seemed like big somewheres. One day Gerry took me for a ride to the center of town and back; another day he took me to the nearby town where I grew up; we walked around the common and stopped by the farm I lived in so I could take a picture. What a wonderful outing it was ... but, of course, we couldn't go inside the village store to see if it's still the same as when I was a kid and we couldn't visit with anyone. The somewheres were accompanied with the underlying warning message always reminding us to --*Keep away from people. Don't touch anything.* Home was safe, the outside world held the evil virus. One wise friend told us the only way to be safe -- *Pretend everyone has the virus.*

Sign on church

People who went to work felt pretty good about it; what may have been a daily chore suddenly felt very special, they knew they were "essential" and that's a pretty good way to feel about yourself and the work you are doing ... even though you're suddenly having to be cautious to stay at a safe distance from your fellow workers.

Life took on a new perspective for everyone. We began to realize and appreciate things that were always available. Toilet paper for example -- Some reflected that we may have to resort to using pages from catalogs as our ancestors did when they went to the outhouse; maybe in our time we could also add paper from junk mail. One friend told me about an amazing surprise given to her on Easter. When she picked up her Take Out meal from her favorite restaurant it included -- a roll of toilet paper! Never before would a restaurant have considered giving toilet paper for a gift and never before would it have seemed a sweeter gift than a piece of chocolate.

The only way to have a restaurant meal

Beauty salons closed, and with all the hairdresser and barber shops closed, we were rapidly becoming a long-hair generation. My thinning hair gets straggly when it's long so I always have a short hair style. My neighbor who has nice thick hair was facing a problem too, "My hair will soon be the color of yours." Her beautiful blond was becoming gray. Manicurists also closed shop. One woman said that her acrylic nails looked terrible growing out, too long for her to be able to use the computer, so she pulled them off and her nails underneath were very soft after not being exposed for so many years. Another friend said her nails only had color left on the tips. The pandemic was certainly revealing our natural selves. Gerry used to recite a cute little couplet if I put on lipstick.

Paint and powder, powder and paint
Makes a woman what she ain't.

Schools. Sports events. Weddings. Showers. Funerals. Parties. Graduations. Churches. Clubs. Jobs. Businesses. Movie theaters. Play houses. Residential homes. Hospitals. Everything everywhere was affected. Signs proclaimed; Closed. No Visitation. Postponed. Cancelled.

A boy asked his dad, "What's the weather this weekend?"
Dad replied, "It doesn't matter -- you're not going anywhere."

A new term entered our vocabularies -- Zoom! In our over 80 years, technology has added a lot of new words to our vocabulary and new definitions to old words -- google, online, app, email, text, facetime, facebook, download, upload, software, hardware, laptop, desktop, scan, skype, mouse, floppy disk, keyboard, hard drive, monitor, iPhone, iPad, and on and on. Wow! That's a lot of new words; it shows how technology has entered our lives and changed them. (Google is Gerry's favorite computer friend; it answers every question he has in an instant and even leads him to YouTube sites that show him how to do things; no more encyclopedias.) But now Zoom has entered the world big time, and people can use their cell phones and computers right from their own homes and see and talk with people in other locations. And, I hear there are other servers that provide the same function. Absolutely amazing!

Zoom has been available from Apple since 2013 and its use has increased by over 1,200% in the past month. We never heard of it before the pandemic, but we are sure it will be here to stay. Businesses and personal use of it will become the new easy way to work with a group, even with people living in distant parts of the world.. Our nephew tells us how he participates in meetings that include people from Europe and Asia: it saves them from having to travel great distances but the meetings for him in California are usually held between 2 and 5 A.M. to accommodate the time differences. Another friend told us about a Zoom Easter family gathering of siblings, her children, nieces and nephews, and grandchildren who lived in various states from Maine to California. They could see and hear each other perfectly and everyone maintained quarantine. Isolated, far apart, yet together. Since the quarantine started, our Bible study group has met the same way every Monday evening. Some things on the computer are not easy to use, but Zoom is, and if Gerry and I can do it, anyone can.. (If my grandmother could come back, she wouldn't recognize the way we communicate today. Just walking around talking into a cell phone would be a shock to her. How far we have come in the 48 years since her passing. With the way technology is developing, maybe one day I'll be able to contact her in heaven?)

Zoom class screen shot of folk dancing with teachers Liz Haraksin and Ben Kwan with 4th graders on Fuzzy Friend Day

Technology was quickly put into service. How else would school kids be able to complete their classes and be promoted or graduated? Online teaching, which had been used mostly on the college level, was quickly put into use for all school levels, elementary through high school, as well as in colleges. Incorporating it has been a challenge for schools and teachers who had never done it, also for kids in the primary grades; older kids are computer savvy and picked it up quickly. For most teachers, it meant planning lessons in a whole different way as well as learning how to use the software. One teacher told how chaotic it was when all the kids answered a question at the same time before she learned how to use the mute button that allowed her to have them speak one at a time, also she could see the order in which students pushed the answer button and called on them in order. She said lesson planning took a lot more time than it had before. One teacher said the virus is responsible for her learning so much technology.

Another teacher friend taught in a school that didn't have a way to access the students by computer; teachers in her school called the students on the telephone, and every student was to be called three times a week. What a task, individualized teaching!

Using the computer was easy for high school students to continue their classes, but for seniors, school closure meant missing the activities they had looked forward to for four years -- the prom, field trips, senior week with its awards and cookouts and culminating with graduation ... no wonderful week of fun, festivities, and farewells.

Masked seniors holding a precious gift --
toilet paper wrapped in the school color with 2020 on it

Furthermore, their minds were full of college plans -- worry, will the virus be ended by fall when college starts, will they be able to start on target. What was ahead? Some students felt depressed, many felt angry. And you can't blame them. Finishing high school is a crossroads in life, an emotional time anyway as one moves from childhood to adulthood, and now the road ahead had no clear path.

One senior told me she's trying very hard to have hope. She's trying to adapt to the situation, knowing the school administrators are doing the best they can. She said, "It makes me look at life differently and be grateful for what I have and be thankful that none of my friends or family have the virus." I told her that with a positive attitude like hers, she will do well in life. When we can't change a bad situation, the only thing we can change to make a big difference is our attitude about it.

A young man in our town was selected to be the recipient of a prestigious award from his college for his outstanding scholarship in government. The event had always been held in a formal ceremony at the college every year with relatives, friends, and professors there to share and recognize the excellent achievement and promise of the scholar in a field the world needs. However, with quarantine in effect, what was the college to do? They didn't want their high achievers to go unrecognized. Zoom was the answer. It was effective, each scholar was recognized individually and the qualified students will receive their certificates and awards later in the mail, but you could feel the remorse in the professor's voices that the candidates could not be together to share the special moments and afterward socialize at a reception. Change and adapt was the order of the day, but do our best not to neglect. One thing I often think about are the stories these young people will have to tell their grandchildren.

Postponed: I'm old fashioned so I don't think a wedding postponement today would affect a couple as much as it would have in my day, 58 years ago. Most couples today live together before they get married, which I am not criticizing as time does change lifestyles, so these people about to be married can just continue living as they have been; it is only disappointing having to postpone the celebration with friends and family in making their relationship with each other a formal lifetime commitment. In my day, it would have meant living apart for a longer time. (I just heard about one couple who have moved their wedding ceremony ahead 1 1/2 years!) Perhaps if this had happened to us, we would have started the "living together" idea sooner. I wonder if anyone has had a wedding ceremony on Zoom??? (I did attend an Internet funeral, and the man who died would have loved it. He was 95 and one of the first to bond with a computer.)

All these postponements (weddings, showers, birthday and anniversary parties) present a huge loss of business for the facilities that host them and also a big complication for everyone in rescheduling ... and when will it be safe to reschedule. So many unknowns.

Our lives are steered by uncertainties,
many of which are disruptive or even daunting.
Amor Towles

The virus is most deadly to the elderly, and reports reveal the high toll on residents in nursing homes where everyone is living close together. One worker said, "It spreads even though residents are kept isolated in their rooms and the staff workers all wear protective gear and heavy duty masks. It is so emotional to watch how quickly the virus takes them down." Another said, "It's so tragic. We are losing our senior generation." One of my best friends lost her brother in a veterans' home, he was one of the many to succumb to the virus there.

And funerals. What should be done about the loss of a loved one? In an attempt to keep out more germs, hospitals and nursing homes didn't allow visitors so when people died there, they died without loved ones at their sides. Sad for them, sad for loved ones who couldn't have closure, and then having the dilemma about how to have a funeral service when a group can't gather. What to do? Wait? Have it later? When? Have a service on Zoom? All these questions magnified the grief for loved ones. And, what about the job of undertakers who have to handle bodies that perished from the virus?

Gerry having a telemedicine visit with Dr. Gretchen Kelley

Sports events and entertainment. Yes, we did miss them. They are our pleasure outings -- a time when we leave our daily thoughts and cares behind, a time to see performers we admire. We missed those opportunities. But, the pandemic made us think about other performers, ones that didn't make as much money, ones not out there in the limelight, but they are the people who are out there risking their lives to serve and save others -- The Frontline. They became the heroes in our lives, the performers we admired. More than ever we appreciated doctors, nurses, EMTs, police, firemen, truck drivers, postal workers, and grocery workers. Even the services of the National Guard were on duty. Our neighbor put a sign on the tree by the roadside -- "FRONTLINE, Thank You". Yes, thank you, thank you from the bottom of our hearts.

Tribute to the Frontline

Churches have done a wonderful job in using online services. Some churches had already provided that service for shut-ins. Suddenly, everyone was a shut-in and church pastors found a way to reach their people. (It amazed me that computers weren't overloaded with so many people and institutions using them. Computers meant connections.) People needed the uplifting messages and promises of their faiths more than ever.

Our minister kept her parishioners connected by sending emails with spiritual messages along with updates on the happenings and needs of our church family. On Easter Sunday, a loud speaker system was set up in front of the church and we parked our cars around the town common and stayed in them to hear the Easter message; though safely separated, we were together and felt together. An inspiring and uplifting experience. A message had been placed in the announcement box on the side of the church -- "Stop the Spread." The message of Easter was another kind of "spread" -- "Spread the Word."

Drive-in church service

Many people are doing their parts to telephone, text, email, snail mail, facetime, etc. to spread words of support, and whether the messages were spiritual or emotional or newsy, people were spreading important words that said, "I care."

Kindness blossomed like never before. A younger friend told us, "I will do your shopping and errands. You two are in the high risk bracket. You need to stay home." When we talked with our elderly friends, they too had good Samaritans helping them. Kindnesses were spreading. Our neighbor, who is a hunter, said they had a lot of game in their freezer and he and his wife cooked a delicious healthy meal every week for the old folks in the neighborhood -- and left them safely by the backdoor. The delicious meals were so much appreciated; they were seasoned with love, the best kind of spice.

Neighbors delivering Saturday night supper

We began to realize there were some benefits to old age and I could see that the givers seemed to feel as good as we who received their outreaching. I remember many years ago our minister saying, "If you feel down, do a good deed for someone and you'll feel better." Everyone was down at this time, how could you not be with all the heartbreaking reports we heard every day? Everyone knew someone who was struggling with some consequence from the virus.

" Nurse Elaine," showing the emotional aspect of this time.
Drawing by her sister Amelia Ickler

Everyone felt fear, fear for their lives and lives of loved ones, discouragement about the economy, and loneliness from the social isolation. One problem I had, a small problem, but I heard others mention it too, was keeping track of what day of the week it was. Every day had become the same. Stay at home, talk on the telephone or email, listen to the news and hope the situation was improving. We weren't just "shut-ins", we were "shut-outs". A shut-in can receive visitors, a shut-out cannot go out or have someone come in. Even the Japanese in internment and lepers could visit with each other. Prisoners in solitary confinement -- that's what we were. We longed for warmer weather when we could go outside and visit from a safe distance. (It won't be a comfort for someone with a hearing problem.)

It was the caring acts that saved us, and it was good to hear them broadcast every day. People were thirsting for uplifting news rather than scandal and sensationalism. Seamstresses were making masks for friends and healthcare facilities; car companies started producing ventilators for hospitals; government stimulus checks were sent to give people financial support during this crisis; the income tax return date was extended; generous donations were made to the food bank; some landlords waived a month's rent. People who could afford it were reaching out to make life easier for ones who were adversely affected by the pandemic. The caring list grew longer every day.

I was amazed at how quickly virus jokes started appearing on the Internet. Smiles are healthy. One friend emailed a question, *Anyone else's car getting three weeks to the gallon?* It made us stop and think about how seldom our car left the garage. In fact we received a notice from our insurance company stating that their customers will be receiving a refund. Of course, accidents were down with so few cars on the road.

The United States wasn't facing this crisis alone. Everyone in the world faced the same situation. We were all in this together, everyone in our country, everyone in the world. We all felt for each other, we were joined. It was no longer just the United States we were living in, it was the United World. One friend said, "Maybe this was what it takes to unite the world." On Easter the Pope delivered a loving message of peace and unity:

We are all in the same boat -- all of us are called to row together -- each of us needs the comfort of each other -- only together we can get through this -- we need to be like brothers and sisters -- our planet is gravely ailing -- this time of trial is a time to get our lives back on track -- God will bring serenity into our storms.

We heard families talking about enjoying each other, having time together, playing games, taking walks, enjoying nature. Little kids loved being with their parents all day, rather than with a babysitter. People were connecting with old friends they hadn't seen or talked to in a long time. Reminiscing became an important topic of conversation, nostalgia, something we don't give enough time to, conversation about people and times that were good, it gave good relief from the virus news -- the only news.

Interestingly, one friend said her dog was having a hard time with the family being home all day. Usually he had the house to himself and slept all day; his family fun came in the evening and the change upset his appetite. Another friend happily reported a change in the family meals. Both he and his wife had full busy work schedules and she often picked up a take-out meal or they fixed something quick and easy. When her company closed and she stayed home, her husband had a pleasant surprise after all those years and announced, "She can cook!"

Our perspectives will definitely change because of this tough time. We will be more thankful for our families,, our neighbors, our community and the frontline people. We will observe and better appreciate nature. We will be better planners, and more conservative with the items we use -- especially toilet paper. With courage and perseverance we will get through this, and with faith and new goals, we can unite and make the world a better place.

There was nowhere to go but we learned good lessons and viewed life differently ... and that took us somewhere important. From every experience we have an opportunity to grow.

My Only Up-close Friends

When people ask if all I do is talk about chickens, it's like;
I'm supposed to be talking about something else?
Raising Happy Chickens.com

Ain't nobody here but us chickens
Louis Jordan

Distancing was the order of the day. Six feet. Most of the time people stayed even further away. Fortunately for me, I had Gerry to be close to, and we both had good hearing so we could communicate with neighbors at a distance, knowing we would do it more often when the weather became warmer. However, during this period I did make a dozen new unexpected friends that I could be close to and they brought me joy every day.

Our neighbor Rick welcomed us to gather eggs from his chicken coop, a generous offering we have been blessed with since we downsized and moved to our small retirement home 25 years ago. We are not big egg eaters. Gerry has a heart condition and through the years health reports said eggs were high in cholesterol so we became cautious, then later we read they were great whole-food items. What to believe? We decided to go with the wise advice -- "everything in moderation" and enjoy a good meal with eggs without any feeling of guilt. Gerry is 88 so I guess the suggestion of using moderation were good words of wisdom.

When we walked by the pen attached to the coop in the summer, we picked handfuls of grass and clover and tossed it to them. They grew to expect those offerings and ran to the fence when they saw us passing by. I loved to listen to their contented voices as they quickly consumed the greens.

Most days when I take my walk I notice every plant I pass and hear every bird that sings, on other days I walk to settle some question or deep thought on my mind and I don't see anything. On one such day, I walked right by the chicken pen and didn't give them their usual handful of grass, and when it became obvious to the chickens that they were being neglected, they made loud squawking noises, harsh reprimanding calls that awakened my attention to them. I quickly returned and gave them their usual snack. It made me realize that chickens are smart.

Well, when the pandemic came and we were quarantined, I started to really discover what interesting characters these chickens are. Most farms have all red chickens or all white ones, all chickens of one breed, but Rick has an assortment of breeds so they don't look alike and it became possible to distinguish one chicken from another. Also interesting were the eggs. When you buy eggs from the store, you get a carton of white eggs or one of brown eggs, but not so from Rick's chickens. Because they are a variety of breeds, they lay eggs in a variety of colors -- white, varying shades of brown, some even blue; our carton of eggs looks like an Easter variety.

I had always gone into the chicken coop about once a week to gather the eggs I needed, but with no friends to visit, no church meetings, no services to attend, no historical society programs to go to, no museums to visit, no trips to see children or grandchildren, no one to invite for supper or to visit at their homes for supper, no visits to Gerry's doctors, who could I visit? Solution --I made new friends -- chickens. Because life slowed down, instead of once a week, I started collecting eggs as I used them, one or two at a time, and I didn't just pick them up and leave, I started spending more time there and observed that each chicken, like people, had its own individual personality..

Some of the chickens started to allow me to pat them when they were in the nesting box where they lay their eggs. One black and white one that I call "Zebra" even liked being stroked so much that she jumped up onto the rail in front of the boxes and walked back and forth to get patted each time she passed; she'd never gotten brave enough to just stop completely.

I started to enjoy the little creatures so much, I decided to visit them every day, not to get eggs but just to visit and I brought them little treats -- like apple peelings and the outside leaves on lettuce and cabbage. At first I tossed the snacks on the floor and then I started offering them from my hand. Zebra reached up with her beak and snatched them right away. The others were a bit reluctant but observed her and one by one they learned I was a safe feeder and reached for their snacks too. Among the brood of about a dozen chickens is one rooster and it was a victorious day for me when he too reached for his tidbit. (He had previously been grabbing bits from his chicken harem.)

Rooster is quite a mellow fellow, but for some reason he plucks out feathers from the back of the chickens in his harem when he does his "thing" ... and he does service all of them because they all have some of their beautiful tail feathers missing. I would think he'd want his girls looking their most splendid best. One of his girls lets him know what she thinks about his plucking actions --- she must have a vengeful spirit because she regularly pecks at his backside ... and he doesn't like it. I think she's trying to reform him by letting him know that it hurts to have tail feathers pulled out. If I could give her advice I would tell her -- It's not easy to change a man!

I always visit after lunch and I think they have a sense of time because as I start up the hill toward the coop, they spot me from their pen and start dashing inside. By the time I get to the door, they are so tightly clustered there that I have to open it carefully and can hardly squeeze in without stepping on them. On one particular day, after they had become well adjusted to taking food from my hand, they backed away when I extended it, seeming a bit scared. I was puzzled. What was wrong? Then I realized that I was wearing green gloves, never before had I fed them with gloves on. I took them off and they happily returned to be fed. Are chickens smart? Are they observant? Their intelligence went up another notch that day!

Feeding chickens

I have two favorites, Zebra and one I call Jackie who will jump to get a bite, which reminded me of a jumping jack so I call her Jackie. She's kind of an orange-brown color and has great spirit. She's always the first one at the door to greet me, Zebra is second. Jackie is eager and smart, but Zebra also has a special attribute -- she talks, very soothing contented-sounding responses when I talk to her. I'm wondering if any others will become talkers and jumpers.

There's only one chicken who makes me feel a little sad. I think there are some chickens, like people, who have special needs. She never follows the others into the chicken coop for food and when you toss some grass into the outside pen, the others get it before she realizes it's there. And when night comes and all the chickens go back into the coop to roost, she doesn't follow.

The chickens go inside when Rick goes down in the evening to close the little door from the pen to the coop so they will be safe from nighttime predators, like owls and raccoons; they know it's time to go in, all of them except the special-needs girl. How does he corral her in? He sends out Mr. Rooster to do it. The man of the coop is in charge ... he takes care of his household!

Gerry smiles when I tell him every day after lunch, "I'm going to visit my friends." I'm sure he thinks I'm a little crazy, but during this pandemic, we all are glad if our loved ones can find an activity to keep them happy. And, for me, I've learned a lot and had fun. I'm thankful. Many senior friends have only one or two people they can be close to during this quarantine. Besides Gerry, I have twelve others, and like all animal friends, they are always happy to see me.

Through the Window

How do you visit a loved one who is in a shut-down facility such as a nursing home, hospital, or group home? You know the "stay-out" policy is for their own safety so virus germs cannot be brought in, and you certainly don't want to be the cause of bringing Covid-19 to someone who probably already has a weakened health system. But you love them and they love you, and loneliness has already become a part of their lives when they had to leave home and go to a care facility when adequate care could no longer be managed at home.

Gerry and I were facing that situation with our special needs son Grant who is 56 and has lived in a group home for past 25 years. He is confined to a wheelchair and had been transported to an excellent day program filled with stimulating activities he enjoyed. He has a TV in his room so he can watch his favorite DVD's. He strings beads to make necklaces for his friends and relatives, and his beading even serves a missionary outreach when our minister asks him to make necklaces to cheer up women who are grieving or having a problem. He uses the telephone to call home and talk to family and call some old friends. We visited him at his group home weekly and a staff person at the home brought him to a nearby restaurant so we could enjoy a meal with him, and often some friends would join us for the meal and fellowship. Grant had a full schedule and was very happy. And, as the saying goes, "A mother is about as happy as her least happy child." I was happy that he had made such a good adjustment.

It's hard to face the fact that it's time to put your child in a group home. You feel guilt, selfish, inadequate, like you're giving up on a person. Even though Grant was in his 30's, the best way I can describe the feeling for me would be like sending a kindergartener off to college. Like a kindergartener, the special needs child is never grown up enough and ready to leave home, not like high school graduates who can't wait to leave and be on their own, although they often do feel homesick after they do leave.

I'm sure it has to feel the same way when it becomes time to put a parent or spouse in a care home. It's not an easy decision and takes mental preparation and adjustment on both sides. Change is one thing that comes to all of us from time to time in our lives.

A BIG change came with the virus, a change that presented most everyone in the world with new challenges. How to bring some diversity to Grant's life was one of our challenges. His day program closed, and not only was he confined to his wheelchair, he was confined to his group home and most of the time in his room. I'm not sure he realizes the impact the virus had on the world but he sure knows it's had an impact on him. All the activities he loved came to an abrupt stop. He calls it the Terrible Virus. Then Gerry and I thought ... Grant lives in a one-story house and his window is low enough for us to look into. Let's visit him from outside through the window. And that's what we've done.

Visiting through the window

Once you accept a situation and find a solution for working with it, you can begin to find ways to make the new method fulfilling. At first, our window visits were pretty much the same as our telephone conversations, but then we added some creativity, and started to do a show-and-tell kind of visit. He held up thank you letters he received from women he made necklaces for and we talked about those people and their lives, and how much joy his necklaces brought to them, reflections that made him feel good about his hobby and that he had more time to work on during this confinement. He also showed us a picture of

Grant showing us painting he made

flowers he painted. We admired it and asked if we could bring it home to display; he was pleased that we wanted it and the staff person put it outside for us to take. We talked about difficulties the virus was making in our lives -- my hair, that I couldn't go to Monique's to have it cut, that it was getting so long and straggly that I asked Dad to cut it because he was the only one I could be near. I showed Grant how Dad cut it longer on one side than the other and needed to work on it some more; we talked about this being his first haircut so it would take some practice to get it right, how every new job takes a lot of time and practice to get it right. At another visit, we talked about the dentist office being closed. I showed him my broken tooth ... right in the front. I told him the dentist will be able to fix it but for now it was a good thing nobody could see me. The window visits were a good solution, and to further upgrade the visits, Gerry brought Windex and cleaned the outside of the window.

I saw a newspaper photo of someone who had a unique idea for having a window visit with a hospital patient on the third floor! An arrangement was made with a contractor who had a bucket truck and the visitor was elevated to the patient's window for an important in-person visit. I'm sure glad Grant is not on an upper story because I wouldn't have the courage to ride in a bucket although it may not be any more scary than a ferris wheel ride. Anyway, not many of us have access to a bucket truck, but it is an inspiration to see ways people have found to meet important needs. Facetime and zoom have been the answer for many of us to have opportunities to see as well as talk with people. Grant can't do that advanced technology so the window visits have been the perfect answer for him.

Fortunately, he can use the telephone. He calls us every day and Gerry and I search for things to talk about. What do you talk about when you don't have your normal active life and the only news you hear about is the virus? We tell him the news we get from telephone calls and emails, news that mostly revolves around the virus, but the most enjoyable conversations for him and for us are nostalgia topics. We reminisce about people and activities from the past. I remember back years ago when my aunt was in the nursing home, the conversation that brought her the most joy was talking with her about the good old days, and I heard interesting family stories that happened before my time. It's important to keep up with current news, but reminiscing is a good remedy for stress about a difficult situation that is beyond our control. It removes us from the present crisis for awhile and that is healthy.

The Terrible Virus

Through the years Gerry made many little books for Grant about episodes and challenges in his life. The goal of these books was to help him face the difficulties his handicaps presented and feel value for the things he could do. Developing good self-esteem is important for every child.

The limitations of the virus presented new challenges for Grant, and Gerry made a book for him to show how he was able to maintain a positive attitude during this period.

THE TERRIBLE VIRUS

Old Mill Closed March 12

Gardner Workshop CLOSED Due to the VIRUS

When the Terrible Virus came, Grant's workshop had to close. The Old Mill restaurant closed too, and Grant was going to celebrate his birthday there with his good friends -- his first babysitters Lucy and Judy. He was SO disappointed.

Dad said, "Don't be upset. It's just postponed. We will go later.

Everyone had to stay home so the Terrible
Virus wouldn't spread. Grant watched
videos with lots of funny disasters that
his friend Kay gave him. And, while he
watched them, he made necklaces. One
was for a girl that Pastor Stephanie told
him about. She was sad that her graduation
was cancelled and Pastor Stephanie said
a necklace would cheer her up.

No one could come into Grant's house,
not even his neighbor Mike, and everyone
liked to see Mike. However, Mom and
Dad found a special way to have visits.
They drove to Grant's house and visited
through his window. They stayed outside
so they wouldn't bring in any germs but
they could see each other and talk.

Grant was very thankful for the telephone. He talked to Mom and Dad for a long time every day, and he got calls from lots of friends -- Lisa, Mrs. Pollard, Susan, Mrs. Cohen, Mrs. McCormack, Judy, Lucy, Aunt Wendy, Aita, and Beth. He kept Mom and Dad up on all the news.

During this time, Grant did very well. He made lot of necklaces, he watched many funny DVD's, he talked with many people on the phone. But, he was anxious for the Terrible Virus to go away! He wanted to go back to the workshop. He wanted Mom and Dad to be able to visit him in his room. And he wanted to go out to eat with his parents and friends.

Appreciation for Today's Angels

We must find time to stop and thank the people who make a difference in our lives.
John F. Kennedy

Angels are spiritual beings who carry out God's work. They are kind, gentle, and protective guardians. They are portrayed as human bodies with wings and a halo and comfort us in times of trouble. Mary saw the angel Gabriel who came to her to announce she would give birth to God's son Jesus. Today many of us, especially we seniors, are seeing angels, not ones with wings and a halo, but ones who are kind, gentle, and protective of us in this time of trouble.

Some forecasters predicted that the coronavirus could wipe out the senior population. And death reports indicated that could come true. Warnings. Stay home. Be safe. How do you stay home and be safe if you don't go out to get your groceries and medications?

Angels, human angels reached out to protect the senior generation. Do these angels like to do extra errands at the grocery store, the bank, the post office, the pharmacy? Not really. Many of them are busy working from home or at essential jobs. Do they feel safe in public wearing a mask and gloves? No, they know the miniscule molecules of the virus may penetrate their masks or get on their clothing. Do they like waiting in long lines for window transactions at the bank and pharmacy? No, they are used to quickly going into the place of business, doing their errand and leaving. Is the trip to the transfer station a quick easy stop to dispose of rubbish? No, it's another tedious long wait in line for your turn, and then when you finally get to the place to drop off your trash you feel hurried to find the right place to deposit the recyclables because you don't want to keep others waiting any longer than necessary. Everything is a reminder of how suddenly life has changed. One person said, "It feels like we're living in a police state with all the regimentation and controls ... but it is good to see that the state and federal governments passed laws that require safe procedures." With all the extra time and effort it takes, are these angels sorry they volunteered to do errands for seniors? No. That's the one thing they wouldn't change. They care. They know how much they are needed and it's fulfilling to be needed.

Gerry and I have an angel in our lives ... our younger friend Karen. When the shut-down started in March, she told us, "You need to stay home. I will do your shopping." She knew we didn't have family members living nearby who could do errands for us. With both of us in our 80's and Gerry recently finishing chemotherapy treatments, I gratefully accepted expecting it would be only for a week or two. I emailed my grocery list to her and she delivered them to the trunk of our car in the garage where I picked them up and brought them into the house.

We always took it for granted that we'd be able to get every item on our shopping list. There were never empty shelves in our grocery stores. Things like that only happened in third world countries. Not anymore. We too began to experience shortages. The virus made us appreciate what the suppliers could provide. Unpacking the bags of groceries began to feel like Christmas. My thoughts were ... Wow, they had pasta this week! They had tomato soup, rice, flour, even toilet paper! Who would ever have expected there would be so much joy in getting the common everyday items that were always available in abundance?

Karen delivering our groceries

As much as I am thankful that we have a guardian angel keeping us safe, a part of me feels I am missing out in experiencing a page of history. I don't see the people lined up six feet apart to enter the store, I don't see the arrows marking the one-way aisles, I don't see the plastic shields on the counters separating the customers from the postal workers, I don't wait in line to do my banking, I don't wear a mask and gloves. The only precaution I have to take is to wipe down the cans and packages as I put them away. I am missing a big piece of history but know it's a good piece for us to miss.

Now here it is more than four months later and Karen is still faithfully doing our errands ... and she has a busy demanding job. I know she has to be as concerned as everyone is about the risk she is taking when she goes to a public place and she has to be frustrated about the increased time errands take, but she continues to do them just as cheerfully as she did the first week.

People feel their best when they are doing something that helps someone or society. Today's angels are valuable, and they make the ones they serve feel valued. They are another category of Frontline people in our lives.

Afterword

Look Inside

The stories about the Japanese, the lepers, and all the ethnic groups who suffered from prejudices in America, brought my chicken friends to mind. Chickens sounds like a strange thing to be reminded of, but there's an underlying reason for that thought.

My neighbor Rick, who owns the chickens and knows about my enjoyment of them, suggested that I try to connect with his peacocks ... and there are five of them -- two females and three males. I always admired them, especially in the spring when the males develop their beautiful long tail feathers and fan them out to create the most spectacular display imaginable. The jewel-like blue in their feathers could compete in a contest with sapphires. They display God's handiwork for sure. But, the peacocks don't lay eggs every day as chickens do; they just lay them when they are ready to reproduce, so I only looked into their pen to admire them when I passed by, there was no reason to enter.

Making friends with the peacocks sounded like a good challenge to have during this isolation time when we needed new outlets to fill our days. Since the chickens responded quickly to my snack offerings, I decided to try the same approach with the peacocks.

They backed away when I entered their pen so I decided to try feeding them from outside by pushing food through the fencing. Mostly, I offered them long blades of grass. They eyed the grass but were shy about taking it even though I pushed it far through the fence holes. Then, I let some stalks drop onto the ground. Slowly, one or two would approach and gobble it down. Great! They would learn how good the grass tastes, a nice change from their usual dry corn and birdfeed, and they will hurry to the fence and take it from my hand. That's what I thought.

For one month I continued the same routine. I don't give up easily. They definitely liked the grass, but were they excited to see me? Did they hurry to the fence to get the grass? Did they begin to feel safe taking it from my hand? No. Our relationship didn't developed much. Occasionally, if the grass extended far enough through the fence, one of them might snatch it, but usually they waited for it to drop and then slowly sauntered over to get it. I had to face it -- peacocks definitely are not the friendly spirited birds that chickens are.

I do like them though. They are not hostile. They are a rather low-key bird, but they do not have a low-key voice -- they make a very loud shrill squawk that can be heard throughout the neighborhood. If you didn't know what it was, the sound would scare you. You wouldn't expect such a beautiful bird would make such a piercing unpleasant sound. Fortunately, they don't call out too frequently. There is one helpful thing about their call -- they are somewhat like watchdogs and usually squawk when a car passes by which gives a good announcement ... or maybe even a warning.

But why am I connecting this bird story to prejudices in America? Well, when visitors come to our house, they pass by the peacock and chicken pens and very often tell us they stopped to admire the beautiful peacocks on their way by, but no one has ever said they stopped to look at the chickens. People don't stop and look at the beauty inside the chickens.

People of different origins also have a different look. We don't stop to see the beauty inside people who have different outside physical characteristics from our own. Prejudices cause us to see beauty only in people who have the same familiar outside look as ourselves, and reject people with different physical characteristics.

With COVID-19 we are all facing the same concerns ... the disease, the economy, the isolation. Everyone is suffering from it in some way.

Can this isolation experience give us a better understanding for the people who have suffered and are suffering from being pushed away and separated -- people who have felt isolated for years? Prejudice. Indians who were relegated to reservations, Blacks who were consigned to a lower class, Polish, Italians, Irish, Lithuanians and all others who came here looking for a better life and only felt secure when they lived in sections of towns and cities with people of their own origins? Many of these prejudices have worked themselves out through time, some have not.

This time of isolation has made me look at some social issues from a new perspective. The protests and outbursts of violence spreading across the country was triggered by pent-up anger against many years of injustice that some police have shown toward Blacks. Perhaps that's a release from the feelings of isolation that prejudice imposed on them.

Can COVID-19 help us to better understand what it's been like for people to be isolated? Isolation is not a subject that's been close to our hearts, at least not as close as it should have been for most of us. It's far away, something we've maybe read about, thought about, then dismissed and gone on with our lives. But, for the ones who have gone through it, and are still going through it, it's made a permanent and hurtful imprint.

This country will not be a good place for any of us to live in unless we make it a good place for all of us to live in.
Theodore Roosevelt

Our attitudes change when we have opportunities to know people of all varieties. I remember back about twenty years ago when I was driving our granddaughter Naomi to a junior high school dance and she asked me to come to the hall to meet her boyfriend whom she said was so cute. She told me to wait at the doorway and she'd go get him. Thoughts of my grandmother jumped into my mind when I saw her walk up to an African American boy and lead him back to meet me . What would Grandma have thought? How would she have handled this? She would have been shocked and angry and worried ... she may have told me to return home with her. I realized that Naomi didn't see color. She saw the nice person inside. She attended school with people of various nationalities and color. She knew them as people, not as a race. I felt so proud of her and thought about what a long way we have come. Time and togetherness makes the difference.

I'm thankful for the African American and Asian friends in our lives, but I'm sorry to say we haven't had an opportunity to develop a friendship with any Native Americans. However, my great grandmother proudly told us we had Indian blood in us. I was young and regrettably didn't ask questions about the lineage, but all my life I've felt good about that heritage.

The following words *Jesus Loves the Little Children* were written by Clare Herbert Woolston over 150 years ago, during the Civil War Era. He was obviously trying to unite all people during the period when we were fighting to liberate slaves. The words were put to music and have been one of the most popular children's church songs. We adults need to sing it too, maybe substituting "the little children" with the word "everybody."

Jesus loves the little children
All the children of the world
Red, brown, yellow
Black and white
All are precious in His sight
Jesus loves the little children of the world.

If Jesus says All are precious, who are we to argue with Him?

CPSIA information can be obtained
at www.ICGtesting.com
Printed in the USA
LVHW020753160920
666056LV00007B/294